us
570

Evel Knievel

Evel Knievel
by Joe Scalzo

A THISTLE BOOK

Published by

GROSSET & DUNLAP, INC.

New York

PICTURE CREDITS: Dennis Greene, pages 12, 17, 34, 42, 50, 53; *MotorCycleWeekly,* pages 2, 19, 25, 28, 32, 39, 45, 56, 61, 64, 70, 75, 76, 80, 83, 87, 90, 93, 94; Harley Davidson, pages 6, 67, 69, 80

Contents

CHAPTER 1

"I'M AN EVEL KNIEVEL"

When he was a little boy, Bobby Knievel went to see an auto thrill show near his home. He watched daredevil drivers jump big passenger cars from ramp to ramp and speed through walls of fire. These were dangerous stunts. But the drivers were well-trained professional stuntmen.

After the thrill show was over, the crowd of several thousand applauded enthusiastically. Bobby Knievel, just eight years old, applauded the loudest of all. Never before had he seen anything so exciting.

The next day at home, Bobby knew what he wanted to do. He took some old wooden doors out of his grandfather's garage. He propped them up with buckets to make ramps. Then, pedaling hard, he attempted to jump his bicycle from door to door.

But the bicycle landed too hard and broke. At first his grandfather was afraid that Bobby was hurt. But Bobby was all right. Then the grandfather scolded Bobby for trying such a dangerous trick. But just as soon as Bobby got a new bicycle, he started jumping it over the propped-up doors all over again.

Years later, Bobby Knievel became the most famous daredevil motorcycle rider in the world, jumping across distances he had never believed possible in those early days. "My most important motivation," he says, "is the urge to be the best. Whatever the cost."

Bobby Knievel was born in Butte, Montana in 1939. Butte is the biggest city in Montana, and is famous for its copper mines, where most of the people work. One day Bobby would work in the mines too.

His parents were divorced when Bobby was only six months old. He was raised by his grandparents. Bobby loved baseball, and as soon as he was old enough he played in Little League. That's where he got his nickname.

During one game, Bobby came to bat and was determined to get a hit. The pitcher stared at him for a long time, but Bobby just glared back. This made the pitcher nervous. He served up a pitch that Bobby knocked clear out of the ball park for a home run.

After this, the other players, and the umpire of the game, nicknamed Bobby "Evil" because of his "evil

9

look." And evil rhymed with his last name, so it sounded good, too.

But Bobby wasn't really "evil." He wanted to do things right. And later he changed the spelling of his nickname to "Evel." He made the nickname his real name. And, Evel Knievel it would always be.

Evel Knievel played a lot of baseball, football and basketball as he grew up. In his spare time, he continued to practice his hair-raising bicycle jumps, just for fun.

When he became a teenager and entered high school, Evel was impatient to succeed. He was confident he would make a success of his life. He had a very positive attitude. "There's nothing that I can't do, if I want to do it," Evel said once.

But Evel was so impatient to succeed that he couldn't wait four years to graduate from high school. So he dropped out of school, and took a low-paying job in the Butte copper mines instead. But quitting high school was a mistake, Evel says now. "Education is so important," he insists. "I did not have much schooling and regret it now."

Working down in the mines was hard, frequently dangerous work. Evel didn't mind it. The work developed his muscles, and at the age of 18 he had already filled out into a husky man. He stood 6 feet tall and weighed nearly 200 pounds. He was not afraid of anything. He was handy with his fists, and liked to box. At arm wrestling he was so strong that there were few who could beat him.

Evel still didn't know what he really wanted to do with his life. He quit the mines to take a job as a truck driver. Then he played semi-professional football and ice hockey. Evel loved

Evel at the start of his career.

violent sports and physical contact. He didn't seem to care about pain. He also participated in rodeos. In winter he went skiing and entered ski-jumping contests.

People in Butte who had watched Evel Knievel grow up, wondered what on earth the boy was searching for. They shook their hands in disbelief. Was he trying to find· some way to break his neck for good?

Evel could not make them understand that what he wanted to do was make a success of his life. And he was searching for the thing he could do best, whatever it might be.

Evel left Butte for two years to complete his army service at Ft. Lewis, Washington. While he was in the army, Evel discovered another sport that appealed to him — pole vaulting. He recalls now that he was able to clear the bar at 14 feet, which was a great accomplishment for a beginner.

When he came home to Butte again, Evel married his old high school sweetheart, Linda Bork. Other men might have been happy to settle down. But Evel Knievel was still desperately searching for something more. He wanted to make a lot of money to support his wife and family.

Evel thought he might earn a good living racing motorcycles. He took out a professional license from the American Motorcycle Association, and entered the slambang world of dirt-track motorcycle racing. Dirt-track racing is extremely dangerous; for one thing, the racing bikes have no brakes. Evel did not mind the danger. He was a very good motorcycle rider. He knew just how to pump the bike's hand throttle while he deftly operated the other controls. And he could do a "wheelie" — ride the

14

motorcycle on its back wheel — for a great distance.

But Evel soon discovered, sadly, that even if he won all his motorcycle races, there still wasn't enough prize money to support his wife Linda and their two young sons. He would have to find still another job. And by this time in his young life he had already had dozens.

The next job Evel tried was police work. He worked for a while as a detective around Butte. Then he worked as an insurance salesman. Then, because he loved hunting and fishing, he worked for a time as a guide and forest ranger in the mountain-wilderness country around Butte.

Evel was now in his mid-twenties. He had had so many temporary jobs he could hardly recall them all. Yet, he was still unsatisfied. He didn't want to be like everyone else. He wanted to be first at everything. "I'm an Evel Knievel, whatever that is," Evel once said, smiling. To some of his friends it seemed that Evel would work at something until he mastered it, but then he would lose interest and have to find something else. And it seemed that Evel wanted to try everything in life that was unusual and dangerous.

Finally, at age 27, Evel made the decision that would bring him happiness, and shape the rest of his life. Recalling the auto thrill show he had seen as a child, Evel decided to form his own thrill show. But he would use motorcycles, not automobiles. He would call the show "Evel Knievel and His Motorcycle Daredevils." Evel firmly believed he knew how to ride motorcycles better than almost anyone. They were special to him. "I always loved motorcycles," he says.

Thinking back to his childhood,

16

Evel always tries to land rear wheel first . . .

Evel recalled how he had jumped his bicycle over the doors he'd borrowed from his grandfather's barn. If he could jump like that with a bicycle, then why not even further with a motorcycle?

But, because he didn't want to be like other thrill show drivers, Evel decided he would have to jump his motorcycle *over* something. He wanted to give people something to remember. Finally he made his decision.

He would jump his motorcycles over a wild mountain lion and a wooden box filled with live rattlesnakes!

Evel performed this first motorcycle jump of his life in 1965 at Moses Lake, Washington. First, he rode wheelies on the bike for the crowd of people who had gathered. Twisting the handlebars of the noisy, bucking

18

... But sometimes he can't hold the front wheel up long enough.

motorcycle, he raised clouds of dust on the dirt field as he skidded the back wheel. He was enjoying himself.

Finally it was time for him to perform the jump. He hadn't practiced it in advance, so he didn't know what would happen. But, because he was Evel Knievel, he was sure he could make it. He signaled his men to put the growling mountain lion in place, and also the crate of buzzing snakes. There was one narrow, wooden take-off ramp, and a landing ramp on the far side of the lion and snakes.

Accelerating and upshifting through the gears of his powerful motorcycle, Evel roared up the ramp and off the end, up into the air. The crowd of people gasped.

Evel cleared the mountain lion but he didn't quite make his landing ramp. The motorcycle's back tire went *crunch* against the box of snakes. The box broke open, and the poisonous critters got loose. But before they could reach Evel, he straightened up the motorcycle and rode away. Then he tore off his helmet and waved happily to the cheering crowd.

Autograph hunters came out of the crowd and pressed close to Evel. He must have signed one hundred autographs. He signed on and on, always smiling. He was happy. He realized that at last he had found the occupation that suited him.

Evel liked the idea of jumping the motorcycle over things. In 1966, he made a jump at Indio, California, on the edge of a desert. But this time he jumped over two parked cars, instead of snakes.

Then, during another 1966 thrill show performance in California, at Barstow, Evel Knievel was nearly killed.

CHAPTER 2

TAKING CHANCES

At Barstow, Evel Knievel stood in the middle of a small county fairgrounds. There were 2,000 people in the wooden grandstands. Evel was getting ready to do a very difficult stunt. At his signal, a rider from his thrill show would ride a motorcycle straight at him. Evel planned to leap into the air, spread his legs, and allow the speeding motorcycle to roar past underneath him!

Knievel signaled. From the other side of the fairgrounds, his helper started the powerful motorcycle, and he rode straight for Knievel.

Evel's muscles tensed. The motorcycle, doing 50 miles an hour, was coming fast.

Evel jumped, and the motorcycle's front wheel barely missed him. But Evel had not jumped high enough. The handlebars of the motorcycle struck him in the groin and thighs.

"I was thrown 15 feet into the air, and my body turned a couple of flips," Evel recalled. "I landed on my back on the ground. I was in no pain, but felt paralyzed. Most of my ribs were cracked or broken. Someone covered me with a blanket. That was the last time I ever tried that particular stunt." Many of the people in the shocked crowd believed Knievel was dead, but he wasn't. Not even the pain of broken ribs could stop him. Knievel returned to Barstow a few weeks later, and put on another show for the people.

But he was almost out of money. It took a lot of money to travel around the country and to pay his seven helpers. Evel's telephone bills were very high, because he made long-distance calls around the country, trying to get people to book his act. But to the managers of the county fairs, amusement parks, and race tracks, Evel Knievel was just another daredevil. His act wasn't special enough.

Reluctantly, Evel paid off his helpers and disbanded "Evel Knievel and His Motorcycle Daredevils." He decided he would try to become a success on his own. But he knew he needed a special stunt, one that would thrill crowds. Then he remembered how he had jumped his motorcycle over two parked cars. No other stuntman or daredevil in the world was doing that.

Evel decided that he would make

A bad landing can really shake you up.

car-jumping his specialty. One day, shortly after his 27th birthday, Evel went to a fairgrounds in Idaho. He was going to try and jump his motorcycle over 13 parked cars and trucks in a row. He set up long wooden ramps on either side of the line of cars. One ramp was for taking off, and the other for landing. This was to be Evel Knievel's biggest and grandest performance to date.

The jump was a disaster. Something went wrong. Instead of clearing the 13th parked truck, Knievel's motorcycle came down on top of it, and Evel was thrown violently over the handlebars.

"I think the motorcyle's chain broke, or a spark plug in the engine fouled, or the engine sucked a valve, I don't know for sure," Evel said later. "When the motorcycle lost power it dropped like a rock. That was it for me.

"I could see the end of the wooden landing ramp coming at me. I saw that baby coming, and I knew this was going to be very bad. Then I crashed down and the bike hit the side of this panel truck.

"Just before I hit it, I closed my eyes and gritted my teeth. I hoped I would wake up afterwards."

Evel woke up afterwards, but his left arm was badly hurt. The accident left a long twisting brown scar there.

"I'm breaking fresh ground as a daredevil and stuntman," Knievel insisted proudly. "I'm setting new standards in the art of motorcycle stunt riding."

Few people had paid much attention to Evel before, but now they began to take interest. No other stunt

27

Evel was just beginning to make a name for himself in 1967. Here he poses with two great motorcycle racing champions: Gary Nixon (9), and Bart Markel (1)

man or daredevil seemed to be taking the chances that Evel Knievel was.

One day in 1967 a reporter went to talk to Evel Knievel. Evel was at the Ascot Park race track in Los Angeles. It was late afternoon. Evel was sweating in the sun. The night before he had jumped over 16 cars. This was a record for him. Now Evel had to load his 40-foot long wooden take-off and landing ramps on a flatbed truck and get moving. He was to make another jump in Seattle, Washington, in three days.

"The big thing about jumping over cars on a motorcycle is to hit the take-off ramp just right," Evel told the reporter. "I don't want the bike's front wheel to hit the ramp too hard. That might throw me over the handle bars. I have to hang on tight. And then I fly through the air and hope for a safe landing."

The reporter wanted to know why Knievel liked to jump. Evel said that jumping was a challenge to him. He had to be the best jumper. Nothing else would satisfy him. "There is only one other person jumping over cars at this time," Knievel said, "but he can only jump over ten of them. And I'm the one who taught him to jump."

Evel said he knew that jumping over cars was very dangerous, but that he did not mind the danger. Danger was merely something he had to live with. And he was being well paid for his stunts. In fact for the first time in his life he was beginning to earn a good living for his wife and children. They lived with Evel in a house trailer back in Butte, but they seldom got to watch him jump. Evel said he didn't want them to watch, because it made them nervous.

"I like to put on a good show for my

fans," Evel added. "I want to show them that I'm the best." He was sure that no one came to his jumps to see him get hurt. "These people are my friends," he said. "They don't want to see me miss a jump, they want to see me make it."

Proudly, Evel showed the reporter his Triumph motorcycle. It had no fenders and no headlights, and it had an engine like that of a racing bike. The engine was loud. It had no mufflers. Behind the seat, where the back fender had been, was a parachute. Sometimes Evel used it to help slow down the motorcycle following a hard landing.

As evening came on, Evel said goodby to the reporter and started out on his drive to Seattle. After Seattle, he had to visit other cities. He was so popular now that people telephoned *him* all the time to hire him.

Into the air on a Triumph motorcycle at the Ascot
race track in Los Angeles.

With some of the money he earned, Evel had been able to buy a Rolls Royce.

But in spite of his success, Evel Knievel was already feeling dissatisfied. This was hard for his friends to understand. But, for Evel, it was the same old story. Once he mastered something, he usually became bored with it. And now that he had mastered car jumping, Evel was looking for a new way to prove himself, and find a new success.

In November, 1967, Knievel was going to jump his motorcycle over another line of cars, this time in San Francisco. He was to be the star attraction at a motorcycle show. Evel wore a red, white and blue leather suit with stars across the chest. He also wore a red, white and blue crash helmet, and a pair of workman's heavy boots.

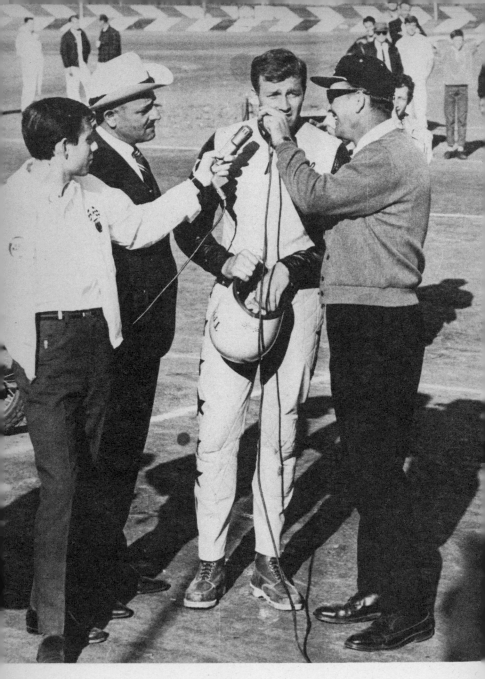

Reporters began to take notice of the
young daredevil.

Evel made a short speech to the waiting crowd. Then he started the motorcycle and warmed up the engine by performing wheelies and other daring feats. finally Knievel signaled he was ready for the jump. He raced up the take-off ramp on the motorcycle.

U.S. 1916367

As he rode off the end of the ramp, Knievel stood up on the foot pegs. This was to give him leverage. He wanted to pull back the handlebars, to lift up the bike's front wheel. This way the motorcycle would land on its back wheel first.

But as Evel stood up, the sudden weight of one of his heavy boots broke off a footpeg. Evel was thrown badly off balance, but he, brought the heavy motorcycle down safely without crashing.

The crowd applauded his skill, and Evel waved back happily. But he was a little shaken. It had been a close call.

A little later that year, Evel appeared on a television talk show to announce his next daredevil stunt. He said it would be the most amazing stunt in history.

"I'm going to jump over the Grand Canyon on a motorcycle," Evel said. "The date will be July 4, 1968."

CHAPTER 3

HOW TO JUMP A CANYON

Evel was pleased with his idea for jumping the Grand Canyon but he was due for a disappointment. The Government wouldn't give him permission to make the jump. Evel had planned exactly how to do it. He may still be able to use those plans some day.

The Grand Canyon crosses Arizona into California. It is 217 miles long and as much as a mile deep. The area of the canyon where Evel wanted to jump was over two miles wide and 3,000 feet deep. At the bottom was the roaring Colorado River.

Explaining how he intended to make the jump, Evel said he would build a giant take-off ramp. The ramp would be 200 feet high and 739 feet long. His specially constructed, streamlined motorcycle would have a jet engine, wings, and a parachute. The bike would be 13 feet long and weigh nearly 2,000 pounds. Evel expected it to reach an astonishing top speed of 250 miles per hour. "It will accelerate from zero to 158 miles per hour in only 3.7 seconds," he added.

The cost of building the giant take-off ramp, plus the jet motorcycle, would exceed one million dollars, Evel said.

"I am going to try and jump across the Grand Canyon," he said, "but I may have to parachute off the bike before reaching the other side. I know how to sky dive with a parachute, and I can 'track' with my

Evel sits still long enough for a publicity photo.

body. If I bail off the bike, I'll just aim my body toward the opposite rim of the canyon, open my parachute, and land there." Evel said that a second parachute would open to carry his jet motorcycle to the floor of the Grand Canyon.

He realized all this was terribly dangerous, Evel said. He could very easily be killed. "If the jet engine on the bike blows up, and the bike starts cart-wheeling into the Grand Canyon, I'm gonna have to have my senses about me. I'll have to know when to parachute out of there. And when I do, my parachute will open so fast, it will put tremendous pressure on my body.

"If I happen to parachute off the bike the wrong way, and open my 'chute wrong, then the motorcycle could come falling after me, and crash right through the top of my parachute. Then I'd fall 3,000 feet to the bottom, and go splat against the Grand Canyon floor. That would be the end for me. No, I don't want anything to do with the bottom of the Grand Canyon."

But in spite of the enormous risks, Knievel continued to prepare for the Grand Canyon jump. He said the U.S. Department of the Interior had given him written permission to make the jump. And, Evel continued, he had offered $100,000 to the tribe of Navajo Indians living on the edge of the Grand Canyon for the use of their land.

Someone asked Knievel why he was willing to spend so much money, and why he wanted to risk his life in this way. He replied that he wanted to jump over the Grand Canyon because no one else had ever done it. He wanted to be first.

Signing autographs after a rough jump.

And, of course, he expected to make a lot of money for jumping. Just the sale of television rights would make him rich, Evel claimed.

"What if you are killed?" Someone asked. "We are all going to die some-day, and I'll just be getting to where we are all going sooner than you," he replied, smiling.

The whole undertaking sounded fantastic. It was hard to believe any-one would want to try such a thing. But Evel Knievel was an unusual person. Evel said he had jet and rocket experts from the country's space program helping him out. These experts, he said, were confident that he could jump across the Grand Canyon. "Some people think I know more about rocket trajectory than any man they've ever met," Evel added proudly.

Many people thought that Evel

Knievel was crazy. But others thought that he was the most adventurous person in the world.

Still other people scoffed, "Evel Knievel will never jump over the Grand Canyon. He's just saying he will, for the publicity."

When Evel heard that, he became very angry. He didn't like people saying he was a phony.

". . . Before I even make the jump," Evel said, "I may show these skeptics I mean business by riding a motorcycle clear across the Grand Canyon on a cable. I'll be just like a tightrope walker in a circus, but I won't have a safety net to catch me. That'd show those skeptics."

But a few months before July 4, 1968, some unexpected problems developed. Evel said that the Department of the Interior had withdrawn its permission and did not want him

Evel loves kids. He has two sons of his
own.

to jump over the Grand Canyon after all. And Evel said that the Navajo Indians did not want him to jump on their land either. He had to call off the Grand Canyon jump.

Evel seemed very upset. He insisted that he had really wanted to make the jump. He hired lawyers to try and get permission for the jump, but they didn't succeed. For a time Evel threatened to go ahead and do the jump anyway, without permission from the government. But he finally cooled down and changed his mind. "I'll just have to find another canyon to jump over," he declared. "I'll keep looking until I find one." In the meantime, Evel decided to continue jumping his motorcycle over parked cars.

His many fans were as disappointed about the cancellation of the Grand Canyon jump as Evel was himself. By

1968 Evel had thousands and thousands of fans in America and all over the world. Evel, in fact, had become the best-known motorcycle daredevil in the world. And only two years had passed since he had made his first motorcycle jump over the mountain lion and caged rattlesnakes in Washington.

Evel wanted to please his fans, particularly the younger ones, who reminded him of his two young sons. He loved signing autographs. He said, "I am going to continue jumping because grown men come up to me afterwards and ask me to shake hands with their sons. This is something I can't turn my back on."

CHAPTER 4

ACROSS THE FOUNTAINS —ALMOST

The gambling city of Las Vegas, Nevada, was in a state of high excitement. Daredevil Evel Knievel had just arrived!

Evel had come to Las Vegas to try the most dangerous and spectacular jump of his career. He intended to cannonball a motorcycle across the water-filled outdoor pools and fountains of the Caesar's Palace casino. The distance across the fountains was almost half a city block.

Evel carefully positioned his take-off ramp between two tall green cypress trees at the edge of the splashing fountains. Far across the water was his landing ramp. Evel squatted down to calculate distance. After a few moments he went back and repositioned the take-off ramp. Still not satisfied, he repositioned it again, moving it a couple of inches. His life depended on the ramps being positioned exactly right. After a few more adjustments he had the two ramps just where he wanted them.

A large crowd had gathered to watch the jump. They pressed close to the fountains, gawking at Knievel and his motorcycle. Evel had modified the bike especially for this jump. Knowing it had to be very strong, he had reinforced the rear suspension and front forks. To make sure he had enough speed to clear the fountain, he had put special cams, pistons and valve springs in the engine. He knew every

A super-wheelie in the streets of Los Angeles.

detail of the bike, right down to how many ounces of air were in the tires.

"When I jump," he had explained earlier, "I stand or lean forward on the balls of my feet. The motorcycle has a tendency to buck and come over backwards on me. So I try and lean forward to hold it down. I want to go off the take-off ramp right at the top of the power curve. If I do, the bike'll go straight through the air. If I don't, the motorcycle has a tendency to drift sideways and cross up."

Obviously Evel was risking his life by jumping over the fountains. But he did not seem to care. "I never get nervous," he said. "But if I do, I don't let anyone know it."

Next, Evel buckled on his brightly painted crash helmet and walked to the motorcycle. The crowd was quiet.

They kept looking at the fountains, and then looking back at Evel.

Evel kicked the motorcycle to start it. A murmur swept through the crowd. Evel could not hear it because he was revving the powerful engine, listening to it carefully. It sounded fine to him. Nodding his head to the crowd, he let out the clutch and the motorcycle started moving fast for the take-off ramp.

At 70 miles per hour, Evel Knievel shot straight up the ramp . . . and then out into the sky!

Up, up, the motorcycle soared. At one point during the spectacular flight, Evel must have been almost 20 feet above the fountains. He sailed like a bird. He was standing on the motorcycle's footpegs for balance, gripping the handlebars and leaning slightly forward. His eyes were staring straight ahead, and he was aiming the

The start of Evel's ill-fated jump at
Caesar's Palace, Las Vegas.

heavy motorcycle for the landing ramp.

CLUMP, went the motorcycle's rear wheel as it came down hard against the wooden ramp. Evel had jumped the fountains and made a perfect landing!

But he had also misjudged his speed, and allowed the motorcycle to land too fast and too hard. The terrific force of this tore the handlebars from Knievel's grasp. With nothing to hold on to, he was thrown from the bike. He felt himself flying through the air, and then his leather-jacketed body struck the ramp with great force and rolled off onto the hard pavement. At the end of the pavement was a brick wall. Evel smashed into this almost head-first and immediately lost consciousness.

When he woke up again, he was disgusted. He had been taken to a Las

Vegas hospital. Evel hated hospitals. Doctors told him he was badly hurt. They said he had broken his hip, pelvis and several ribs. Also, he had a concussion from hitting the brick wall with his head.

But Evel couldn't stand being cooped up inside a hospital and he left, even though he had to stay in a wheelchair for a while.

"I don't like hospital food," he said, smiling. "If you are hungry enough I guess you can eat it. But I'm a New York steak-and-lobster-tail man myself. You don't see much of that in hospitals. They don't seem to go much for oysters Rockefeller either."

Evel insisted he would start jumping again as soon as he could climb out of his wheelchair. And he did. At Scottsdale, Arizona, he tried to jump over 15 parked Ford Mustangs. He did not make it, and in the crash that

Evel and sportscasters Don Meredith (in hat) and
Howard Cosell.

followed, he broke his lower right leg and fractured a foot.

A little later, in early 1969, Knievel broke his left hip and shoulder again. He said that doctors had to insert metal screws in his bones to hold the ends together.

Evel admitted he was in pain, but shrugged it off and said he was used to pain. "I've been racked up so many times that broken bones or arms mean nothing to me any more."

He even seemed able to laugh off all the injuries. "All the metal screws in me keep twisting whenever I land after a jump," he joked. "Since 1967 I've had twelve major open reduction operations. That's when they cut you open and put a plate or a screw in. I suppose I've had about thirty-five or forty screws put in me, to hold the bones together. I'm always in and out of hospitals."

Even though he had hurt himself many times, Evel Knievel claimed he had a great success record. "I've only 'lost it' on 13 of over 200 jumps. That's a 94 percent success ratio," he declared proudly.

CHAPTER 5

FORTUNE AND FAME

Evel Knievel had started his jumping career riding Norton motorcycles. Later he had signed to ride Triumphs. As 1970 started, he was riding American Eagle motorcycles.

The president of the American Eagle company, a man named Jack McCormack, praised Knievel. "He is the best there is. I have a great respect for him. I am sure Evel knows just what he is doing."

McCormack signed Knievel to a rich contract. Owners of the race tracks and parks where Evel appeared paid the daredevil still more money. Evel said that he never jumped for less than $7,000. Since he was now jumping nearly 50 times a year, he was obviously making a lot of money. Evel saved some of it, and made sure that his wife and children had a good life. But Evel also liked to buy expensive things. He had a Rolls Royce, and a Lincoln Continental. He flew his own small airplane. He wore a 10-carat diamond and sapphire ring. From his earlier leg injuries he had a limp, and often used an antique cane with a solid gold head. Back in 1883, the cane had belonged to the mayor of Philadelphia.

Evel said he was thoroughly happy, in spite of all the injuries he'd suffered. He scoffed at those who claimed he had a secret wish to kill himself. "I love life so much," Knievel declared enthusiastically, "that I can't

A good take-off. Evel is holding the front wheel well up.

An antique cane helps Evel overcome a limp from an old leg injury.

wait to get up in the morning. In fact, I go to bed at night bursting with ideas." And Evel had become so famous, that a movie based on his life and called *Evel Knievel* was to be filmed. It was to star George Hamilton and Sue Lyon.

But in spite of his wealth and fame, Evel Knievel refused to slacken his break-neck life style. "Fast living is my way of life," he smiled. During 1970, he intended to make more jumps than ever before.

In January, Evel arrived in Daley City, a San Francisco suburb, to jump inside a large stadium. The usual huge crowd of fans turned out to applaud. Evel used the public address system to thank them for coming, then went to his motorcycle.

Suddenly, the performance was disrupted. Several members of the notorious Hell's Angels motorcycle gang had come onto the floor. Shouting and cursing, they tried to stop Knievel from jumping. One of them threw something at Evel.

The daredevil lost his temper. He left his motorcycle and waded into the Hell's Angels, fists flailing.

Evel was outnumbered, but he didn't care. His fans cared, though. They were furious at the Hell's Angels, and jumped down from the bleacher seats to help. When police managed to break up the fight, two Hell's Angels had to be hospitalized. Knievel wasn't hurt at all.

Composed again, and showing no signs of having been in a fight, Evel returned to his motorcycle. He started it up and made the jump. Then he paused to sign autographs before racing off to Seattle, Washington, where he was booked to jump next.

But he had trouble here, too. Evel

tried to jump over 18 cars. But, as at Caesar's Palace two years earlier, he had a bad landing. This time a rear tire blew out just as he landed, and the motorcycle swerved and skidded for a great distance. Evel stayed with the bike, and saved it from crashing, but the experience had shaken him. He sat silently on the crippled machine for a long time.

On May 10, again in Washington, he wanted to jump over 13 soft-drink trucks. Because these high-bodied trucks were taller than cars, Evel had to build steeper take-off and landing ramps. Again, he had trouble with his landing. This time he was thrown over the handlebars of the motorcycle, and broke his collarbone. He still didn't like hospitals, but this time he stayed in one for a couple of days. "I do need the rest," he sighed. So far, it had been a grueling year for him.

Soaring like a bird over parked trucks in California.

A little later, jumping in Pennsylvania, he injured his back. Some fans were afraid that he had lost his touch as a jumper.

Then, on July 12 in Eugene, Oregon, Evel proved he could still do it. He jumped successfully over 13 parked Pontiacs. At about this time, Evel switched over from his Eagle to Harley-Davidson motorcycles. He arrived at Daytona Beach, Florida, in 1971 to make a guest appearance at a motorcycle show.

"My bikes are Harley XR-750's," Knievel said. "I've got 60 horsepower to the rear wheel of the bike. It's the most powerful set of wheels going. I can go from zero to 60 in four and a half seconds. I should be moving between 94 and 96 miles an hour when I hit the take-off ramp."

Evel had driven to Daytona in a special and magnificent truck, the

Evel and his Harley
Davidson.

longest vehicle of its kind in the
world. Custom-built by Kenworth of
Kansas City, Missouri, it had a 14-
speed Allison automatic transmission.
Evel had his office, dressing room and
lounge in the truck. It included a
color television, stereo, air-
conditioning unit, heating systems,
and Olympia beer on tap. It cost
$99,000.

Stacked neatly in the rear were Knievel's Harley-Davidsons, along with eight tons of take-off and landing ramps. And inside the cab of the beautiful red, white and blue truck, Evel had put a wooden plaque with the hand-carved words: "The people I care about are the people who take risks." Evel said, "Where there's little risk, there's little reward."

After the Daytona motorcycle show, Evel went to Ontario, California, and jumped over 19 cars. He said he was paid a whopping $40,000 for doing it.

Also in 1971, Evel announced his newest plans. He was still upset that his Grand Canyon jump had been called off. But now he had found a new jumping place — the great Snake River Canyon, near Twin Falls, Idaho. He'd leased 300 acres of land there, he explained, so that no one could stop him from jumping. Soon

68

Evel and one of his rocket powered bikes.

he would begin construction of a gigantic 40-degree take-off ramp some 108 feet long.

The vehicle he planned to jump with would be a "Harley-Davidson equipped X-2 Sky Cycle" with 6,000 pounds of thrust. "With my Sky Cycle," Evel said, "I can get up to 350 miles per hour in six seconds." In those six seconds he expected to be 2,000 feet above the Snake River Canyon.

To steer the 17-foot long missile,

Knievel said he would be strapped flat on his belly and would use a pair of handlebars. The lightweight hull would be hand-made out of aluminum. It would have wings, a windshield, a parachute, and an eight-foot shock absorber lodged in the nose. Knievel estimated its value at $125,000.

Evel was uncertain of the exact date of his Snake River Canyon jump, but assured his fans, "I won't stop jumping until I'm forty."

But others wondered if Evel would live that long. In 1972 he experienced another hair-raising accident, this time at the Michigan State Fairgrounds in Detroit. He barreled over the rooftops of 13 cars, but then he and his Harley-Davidson slammed into a concrete wall. But Evel walked away unhurt.

At Atlanta, Georgia, again trying to

Evel wheelies.

jump 13 cars, he injured himself while practicing. Afterwards he was too sore and stiff to jump, and instead did a dazzling series of wheelies, making the bike's engine roar. But people still wanted to see him jump, and they booed their disappointment.

Evel seemed crestfallen at this reception. Finally, shrugging his shoulders as if to say, "Well, you can't please everyone," Evel limped back to the dressing room of his truck.

In July, he flew his Cessna airplane to Castle Rock, Colorado, and tried to land right on the racetrack. A wing tip brushed a fence, damaging the wing. After it was repaired, Evel took some time off. He flew home to Butte to be with his wife and children, and to go duck hunting on the Madison river with his father-in-law, John C. Bork.

Out on the rain-swollen river,

Knievel's ten-foot rubber raft suddenly capsized. Evel, and John Bork, and Evel's two sons Robbie and Kelly, were thrown into the fast-moving water. Knievel managed to save his sons and drag them to shore. When he returned to begin a frantic search for his father-in-law in the muddy water, it was too late. The fast water had carried Bork away, and he was later found drowned.

Evel was greatly saddened by this, but there was little time to mourn for he had to make yet another jump. In early 1973 he was going to fly his motorcycle over no less than 50 cars, all of them pyramided on the football field, of the Los Angeles Memorial Coliseum.

The city of Los Angeles welcomed Knievel, and many banquets and press conferences were held for him. For transportation, Evel used a fast

Maserati sports car. He wore a silver mink jacket, worth $8,800, and around his neck were two medallions fashioned from twenty-dollar gold pieces.

"I hope the day I'll die I'll have spent all the money I earned," Evel remarked a few days before the Coliseum jump. "My greatest fear is for some guy who didn't have the guts to carry my shoes across the street, to marry into my family and then inherit all my money."

His jump of the 50 cars had been postponed by rain once. Inside the Coliseum, Evel had set up a narrow plywood ramp painted blue and white. It was 200 feet long. It extended almost to the top row of seats along the wall of the Coliseum's west end. He would speed down this ramp, then hit the take-off ramp on his screaming Harley-Davidson and try to

A night jump.

Before he jumps, Evel always says a few
words to his fans.

clear the 50 cars. Beyond the cars was a landing ramp, then another narrow plywood ramp shooting up the Coliseum's east wall, and out the exit at ground level.

"That ramp is so steep," Knievel groaned one rain-soaked afternoon, "a man couldn't climb it."

With Evel was the promoter, a man named J.C. Agajanian, who had already invested thousands of dollars in advertising Knievel's coming 50-car jump.

"I'm going to try a practice run," Knievel declared suddenly. He ran for a Harley-Davidson which was parked on the Coliseum floor. Polishing the wet tires to dry them, he planted himself in the saddle. Then he kick-started the machine.

Agajanian didn't want Evel to do it. "Evel, it's too wet," he insisted.

But Evel wouldn't listen and rode up the ramp.

Twenty feet from the top his bike skidded, slipped, and finally tumbled down into the empty aisles and seats. Knievel tumbled down with it.

"Don't worry," Evel called, slowly picking himself up, "all I did was break one of my fingers." Then he remounted the bike and rode it down to the Coliseum grass again.

The 50 cars Evel planned to jump had been jammed tightly together by a fork lift. There were 18 rows of them. A restless crowd of 23,764 arrived to watch.

Following a long wait, Evel roared onto the Coliseum floor. He was riding his Harley-Davidson on its back wheel. He was dressed in white leathers with big stars, and with a red and blue waistband. He was also wearing white boots and a cape. He performed some trick wheelstands standing up on the saddle.

He looked up at the rows and rows of people. Evel was 34 years old, wealthy and famous. And he still had enormous pride. Evel wanted everyone to know he was the best. He wanted to assure them that not only was he going to make this 50-car jump, but he was going to jump the Snake River Canyon someday too.

To the Coliseum crowd, Evel said: "You can say a lot of things about a man. You can say that he is a great race car driver, or a not-so-great race car driver. You can say that he's been lucky, or else that he's broke or rich. You can say he drives a big car or a little car. But you can say nothing better about a man than 'His word is good as gold.' " Then he gave the crowd his word that one day he would jump the Snake River Canyon. And

Ready to go...

he said, "If I jump that canyon and I make it, when I land in that parachute I'll drop to both knees and I'll thank God Almighty that I'm still alive. I'll grab a handful of Idaho dirt.

"If I miss and splatter myself against the canyon wall, I'll just get somewhere quicker where you're going someday, and I'll wait for you.

". . . Now it's time for me to do what I came here to do. Thank you."

And Evel climbed aboard the Harley-Davidson. He got the powerful engine going, went to the top of the big ramp and started down. He cleared the 50 cars with ease. And as his motorcycle's wheels touched the landing ramp, he yanked on a cord. Immediately a red, white and blue parachute blossomed. The crowd applauded and applauded.

. . . up and over.

CHAPTER 6

THE VERY BEST

Orange County International Raceway is a drag-racing strip in Southern California. It is next to the busy San Diego and Santa Ana freeways. On the evening of April 20, 1974, the freeways were filled with cars in both directions. A big searchlight probed the sky. Thousands of people wanted to get inside the race track to see Evel Knievel.

Evel was going to jump over ten big Mack trucks.

Evel had a special liking for Southern California. It was where he had made his first car jumps seven years

It's not a bird, it's Evel. Here he clears a dozen Mack trucks.

earlier. Evel had changed. At the age of 34, he was a millionaire and a celebrity. He didn't have to jump ever again. But Evel didn't want to quit.

Parked near the entrance to the Orange County track was Evel's familiar truck. The truck was almost as famous as Evel. It was painted red, white and blue, and had lots of chrome. Printed on the sides of the truck in gold leaf was: "Evel Knievel Enterprises, Inc., Butte, Montana." And: "Snake River Canyon Jump, Twin Falls, Idaho, September 8, 1974."

Inside the truck, in the air-conditioned lobby, Evel sat chatting with some friends. He seemed a little upset. He had just finished reading a newspaper story that said perhaps Evel was too old to be a good jumper any more — that he was no longer the best.

84

Outside, powerful drag-racing cars roared up and down the Orange County strip. Nearly 15,000 excited people sat in the grandstands. They waited patiently for Evel to make an appearance. Many carried Evel Knievel posters and flags, and several wore Evel Knievel tee-shirts. It was a standing-room-only crowd.

The size of the crowd didn't seem to bother Evel. He was used to performing before big crowds, and he was relaxed. But, so far, 1974 had been a dangerous year for him. A month earlier in Wisconsin, the throttle of Evel's Harley-Davidson had come loose in his hand while he was jumping. He had barely regained control and avoided a crash.

And at Fremont, California, only a week earlier, Evel had made an off-balance landing after jumping over the ten Mack trucks. His 250-pound

Harley-Davidson had wobbled badly on the landing and Evel had just managed to straighten it out. He was having a lot of narrow escapes.

Evel said, "I feel that 5 percent of the people want me to die, 45 percent want me to make it, but want to be there in case I don't, and 50 percent are behind me all the way."

Finally, a little past eight o'clock in the evening, Evel excused himself from his friends. It was time for him to go to work. He went to his dressing room and put on his white boots. He zipped himself into a red, white and blue leather suit. Then he put on his familiar cape which had "No. 1" on the back.

Outside, the crowd hushed as the door to the truck swung open. Evel raced out.

Over the public address system the track announcer shouted, "Ladies and

Before jumping, Evel always inspects his
take-off and landing ramps carefully.

gentlemen! Here he is! Evel Knievel!"

The applause and cheers were deafening. The people in the crowd were pressed six deep against the fences to have a better look at the most famous daredevil in history, Evel Knievel. Here and there a flashbulb from a camera popped. Many fans were taking their own photos.

Waving and smiling, Evel moved to the center of the track. He was accompanied by six bodyguards, two in front of him, two next to him, and two behind him. Evel had had to hire them after unruly fans at another track had tried to come over the fences to touch him.

Evel waited for the applause to quiet. Then he stepped up to the microphone. "I want to thank you for coming here tonight," he said. Next he reminded the crowd that he had

88

practically started his jumping career in Southern California.

"I've been in the business eight years," Evel continued. "I've had ups and downs. I even have some gray hair." He paused, and shook his head. "Now some reporters are saying that I've been broken up a lot, and that I am over the hill."

Someone in the crowd called down to him, "No, Evel, You are still the best."

Hearing this, Evel brightened. "I don't care what anybody says," he declared, his voice rising, "I want you, my public, to judge me. I'll let you set the record straight."

There was more applause. Meanwhile, in the background, Evel's men had opened the rear doors to the truck. They rolled out three powerful 750-cc XR model Harley-Davidsons.

"Would you like to see some wheelies" Evel asked the crowd.

This question was greeted by still more applause. Smiling, Evel said, "Okay. But I want you to know, I don't like to ride on one wheel unless I'm doing at least 100 miles per hour."

There were no less than 19 body guards and assistants around Knievel. He climbed on one of the Harleys, and buckled down his white and blue crash helmet. His men gave him a push start, the motorcycle's engine came to life, and Evel sped off down the track.

The track announcer said, "Evel is checking out the area to make sure it's safe. And now, here he comes!"

Evel had the Harley-Davidson up on its back wheel, while the crowd cheered and waved its hands.

Then Evel braked to a stop. He took

91

"...I don't like to ride on one wheel unless I'm doing at least 100 miles per hour."

the microphone in his hands. "Now," he said, "I'm going to do what I call a 'super wheelie'."

Getting the Harley-Davidson up to speed again, Evel maneuvered his body until he was actually standing on the saddle. Then he jerked on the handlebars with both hands, to lift the front wheel off the ground. Still standing on the saddle, Evel did a wheelie at high speed — a "super wheelie." The crowd loved it.

"Evel's really putting on a show," the track announcer yelled.

Now Evel had to jump over the ten Mack trucks. He made a smooth take-off and soared over the trucks for a perfect landing.

"You fans decide," Evel said moments later into the microphone. "I want you to decide if I still deserve to wear No. 1 on my cape."

This time the applause went on and

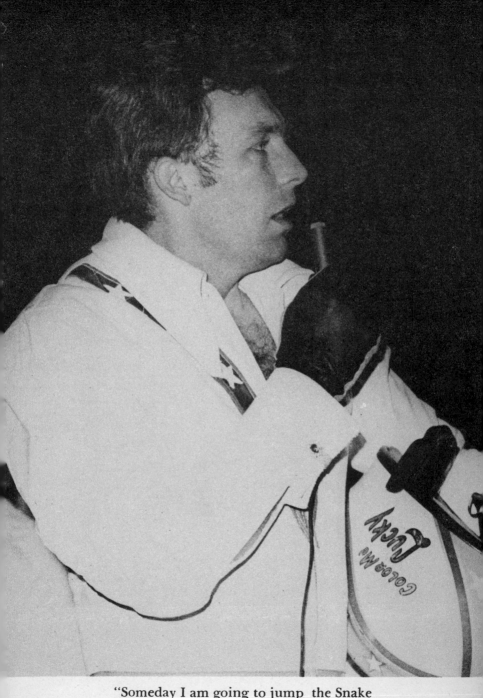

"Someday I am going to jump the Snake
River Canyon..."

on. It made Evel happy. The applause lasted even after Evel Knievel had left the track. His next jump was to be somewhere in the Midwest. And from the mighty sound of the cheering crowd, there was no doubt that Evel Knievel was, indeed, still the best.

A few months later, Evel arrived in Twin Falls, Idaho. At last he was ready for his jump over the Snake River Canyon.

For this spectacular jump of approximately 1500 feet from one wall of the canyon to the other, Knievel would use his Skycycle X-2. It would go up the takeoff ramp at 200 miles per hour. And it would use two rear parachutes as well as the shock absorber in its nose to help it land.

The date of the Snake River Canyon jump was September 8, 1974, a warm and windy Sunday afternoon.

Evel appeared wearing his famous
94

red, white, and blue suit. He thanked the crowd of 30,000 for coming. The people crowded right up to the rim of the 600-foot-deep canyon.

Then Evel got into his Skycycle, and his men helped him get set. The countdown began: 10, 9, 8, 7, 6, ...

At a little past 3:30 in the afternoon, Evel Knievel and his Skycycle blasted off the end of the Snake River takeoff ramp. But some unexpected trouble seemed to develop, and one of the parachutes popped open too early. This slowed the Skycycle in mid-air, caused it to turn, and then slowly drift toward the bottom of the canyon. It brushed against the canyon wall, then landed far below, out of sight of the crowd. Evel Knievel was unhurt.

"I don't know what went wrong," Evel said a little later as the crowd cheered his ill-fated attempt.

He had not made it across the

dangerous canyon, but he had tried. Perhaps he would try again some day. Evel Knievel said, "I have kept my word to myself and to the public."

Evel Knievel jumps into the Snake River Canyon, September 8, 1974.